Reading Essentials®
in Social Studies

U.S. GOVERNMENT

Elections & Political Parties

Carol Parenzan Smalley

PERFECTION LEARNING®

EDITORIAL DIRECTOR   Susan C. Thies
EDITORS   Lucy Miller, Judith A. Bates
DESIGN DIRECTOR   Randy Messer
BOOK DESIGN   Emily J. Greazel
COVER DESIGN   Michael Aspengren

IMAGE CREDITS

© Peter Turnley/CORBIS: front cover; © Brooks Kraft/CORBIS: p. 12; © Jim Ruymen/Reuters
Newmedia Inc./CORBIS: p. 13; AFP/CORBIS: pp. 28–29; Associated Press: pp. 6, 10, 16, 19, 22, 26, 31;
© Paul Blaser/Mark Cady: p. 11

ClipArt.com: front cover, pp. 7, 9 (bottom), 14, 34, 39; Electronic Clipper/Liquid Library: pp. 42, 43;
Library of Congress: back cover, pp. 5, 15, 18, 20, 24; NARA: p. 9 (middle); Map Resources: p. 36;
Perfection Learning: front cover, pp. 27, 40; Photos.com: pp. 8, 21, 41; Public Domain: p. 32

Some images ClipArt.com, Photos.com, NARA, Library of Congress: (Chapter heading bar) pp. 3, 4, 7,
13, 17, 23, 31, 38, 41, 44–45

A special thanks to William J. Miller, attorney, for reviewing this book

Perfection Learning® Corporation
1000 North Second Avenue, P.O. Box 500
Logan, Iowa 51546-0500.
Tel: 1-800-831-4190 • Fax: 1-800-543-2745
perfectionlearning.com

3 4 5 6 7 8 PP 12 11 10 09 08 07

PB ISBN-13: 978-0-7891-6217-5   ISBN-10: 0-7891-6217-2
RLB ISBN-13: 978-0-7569-4186-4   ISBN-10: 0-7569-4186-5

Contents

Elections at a Glance

General Facts

Form of Government   Democracy

Election Day
The first Tuesday after the first Monday in November

First Political Parties
Democratic-Republican Party and Federalist Party

Current Major Political Parties
Democratic Party and Republican Party

Minimum Voting Age   18

> The word *democracy* comes from the Greek words *demos*, meaning "the people" and *kratia*, meaning "to rule."

Timeline of Important Events in the History of Voting

1789	The first presidential election is held.
1828	The first election is held in which there is a popular vote for president.
1832	The first election is held in which presidential **candidates** are **nominated** by national **conventions**.

1840	A presidential campaign uses **slogans**, songs, and campaign materials for the first time.
1870	The 15th **Amendment** to the Constitution prohibits states from denying citizens a vote because of race, color, or prior history as a slave.
1876	Voter turnout is highest in the history of the United States with 82 percent of **eligible** voters casting votes.
1920	The 19th Amendment to the Constitution gives women the **right** to vote.
1924	Voter turnout is the lowest in the history of the United States with only 48.9 percent of eligible voters casting votes.
1936	This is the most one-sided election in United States history. Franklin D. Roosevelt receives 523 **electoral** votes, and Alfred M. Landon receives 8.
1960	This is the closest popular vote in the history of the United States. John F. Kennedy receives 34,221,334 votes, and Richard Nixon receives 34,106,671 votes, for a difference of 114,673 votes. Kennedy goes on to receive the greatest number of electoral votes as well, winning him the presidency.

Campaign badge, 1840

1961	The 23rd Amendment to the Constitution gives U.S. citizens living in the District of Columbia, or Washington, D.C., the right to vote.
1964	The 24th Amendment to the Constitution prohibits states from collecting **poll taxes**.
1965	The Voting Rights Act is passed. It bans states from requiring citizens to take **literacy** tests in order to vote.
1971	The 26th Amendment to the Constitution gives all U.S. citizens 18 years and older the right to vote. The previous minimum voting age was 21.
1984	Geraldine Ferraro is the first woman to run as vice president for a major party. Reverend Jesse Jackson is the first African American to be considered as a candidate for a major party.
2003	For the second time in history, a state successfully **recalls** its governor. The citizens of California remove Governor Gray Davis from office on October 7 and replace him with actor Arnold Schwarzenegger. The ballot includes 135 candidates.

The first recall election in U.S. history took place in North Dakota in 1921. Governor Lynn B. Frazier was blamed for the state's poor economy following World War I. Wheat farmers were especially upset after inflated grain prices dropped sharply in 1920. Frazier was recalled after serving five years as governor. The following year, however, citizens of North Dakota elected Frazier to the U.S. Senate, where he served until 1940.

Chapter 1

Democracy
At All Levels of Government

We live in a democracy. This is a form of government where all citizens have the right to elect government leaders.

The word *democracy* means "government by the people." In a democratic country, each and every citizen can be involved in governmental decisions. As citizens of the United States, we are represented by our elected officials. This type of government is often referred to as a representative government.

Many public officials are people who have been elected to a government position. Their jobs are to serve their communities on a local, state, or national level.

Not all governments allow citizens to elect their leaders or to have representation. Not all countries have publicly elected officials. Many of these governments are ruled by **dictators** or **monarchs**.

Dictator Adolf Hitler

Levels of Government

There are five levels of government. Although it is not an official level of government, the United Nations is a **global** organization to which many countries, including the United States, belong.

United Nations

The United Nations (UN) was established by 51 countries in 1945, following World War II. Its goal is to preserve peace through cooperation between its member countries and to share security resources. Today, 191 countries belong to the UN. It is not a world government, and it does not create laws. It does, however, help resolve conflicts and create international policies for the good of its members.

United Nations headquarters in New York City

The six official languages of the United Nations are Arabic, Chinese, English, French, Russian, and Spanish.

National

The United States of America has a history that started before its official beginnings with its Constitution. The colonies had been ruled by the English **monarchy**. When the United States gained its freedom, the Founders wrote the Constitution to unite the states under one federal government. This document stated that the citizens of each state would choose people to represent them and their interests at the national level.

Preamble to the U.S. Constitution

We, the people of the United States, in order to form a more perfect union, establish justice, insure domestic tranquility, provide for the common defense, promote the general welfare, and secure the blessings of liberty to ourselves and our posterity, do ordain and establish this Constitution for the United States of America.

The United States Constitution

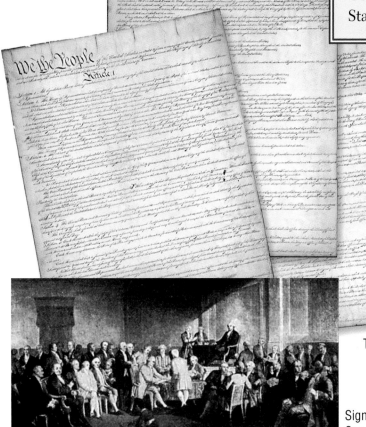

Signing of the United States Constitution, Philadephia, 1787

State legislative session, Madison, Wisconsin

State

The heart of a state government resides at its capital. This is where the governor, state legislators, and other departments run the state. Decisions are made and laws are passed that affect how the state will operate and grow. Did you know that your state's education department helps to determine what will be taught in your classroom?

Local

Cities, towns, villages, and townships have local governments. Usually mayors, city councils, city managers, or other elected officials head these local governments.

Community

Communities can be neighborhoods, housing developments, apartment complexes, or schools. Guidelines and rules are usually set up by **associations**. You may belong to several communities at one time!

You

The most personal form of government is you! As a citizen of the United States, representation begins with your actions—voting, voicing your concerns, being aware of issues, and being an active member of your community.

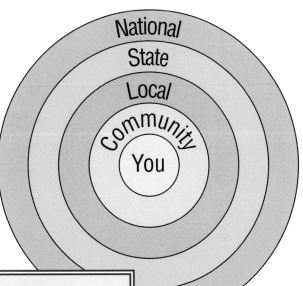

National
State
Local
Community
You

Some Important Elected Offices

President of the United States
Vice president of the United States
United States senator
United States representative
State governor
Members of the state legislature
State attorney general
State comptroller (chief financial officer)
State judges
City mayor
Members of city council
County or town executive
County or town district attorney
County or town judges
Members of the county or town council
Sheriff
Members of the local school board
Members of other local boards or
    commissions

A state court judge

Paying Our Elected Officials

Most elected officials are paid for their political service. While many work full-time in their political positions, others work only part-time. Compare the yearly income of some elected officials and other well-known people.

Steve Jobs, Apple CEO	$219,000,000
Oprah Winfrey, talk show host/entrepreneur	$150,000,000
Tiger Woods, golfer	$69,000,000
Britney Spears, entertainer	$39,000,000
Donovan McNabb, Philadelphia Eagles quarterback	$15,000,000
George W. Bush, president (2003)	$400,000
William J. Clinton, president (1999)	$200,000
New York City mayor, budgeted salary (2003)	$195,000
U.S. senator/representative (2003)	$150,000
New York City firefighter, starting salary (2003)	$33,000
George Washington, president (1789)	$25,000
Small-town mayor, upstate New York (2003)	$8,000
U.S. senator/representative (1815)	$1,500
New York City Mayor Michael Bloomberg, by choice (2003)	$1

George W. Bush and Oprah Winfrey

Chapter 2

Election Basics
Understanding the Democratic Process

Why Vote?

Citizens in the United States vote for government officials.

Voters select representatives at all government levels who have **platforms** or beliefs that are similar to their own. Citizens cannot vote as individuals on each local, state, or federal law being considered. So they choose representatives to vote for them.

However, citizens are involved directly in the decision-making process when they vote on specific projects or concerns, or **referendums**. Most are simple yes-or-no issues. For example, should tax money go toward constructing a new swimming pool in the community? Should money be raised to build a new children's section at the local library? Should a school district build a new middle school?

A woman casts her vote in California.

13

Even though you are not old enough to vote as a citizen of the United States, your voice is already being heard. Does your teacher take a vote on class projects? Does a group that you belong to select youth leaders? If so, you are practicing your voting skills.

Primary Elections/Caucuses

In **primary elections**, one candidate is chosen to represent each political party. For example, five Democratic candidates may wish to run for local mayor, but only one can represent the Democratic Party on Election Day. Each registered member of the Democratic Party can vote for the candidate he or she prefers. The candidate with the most votes will be on the final **ballot**.

In presidential primary elections, people vote for party **delegates** who will represent the voters and cast votes for their chosen candidate at county, state, and national conventions.

Some states do not hold primary elections. They hold special meetings called *caucuses*. Each political party hosts caucuses around the state, giving voters a chance to be heard. Voters at

Registered Voters

When U.S. citizens reach 18 years of age, they can register to vote. Voters can register as Republicans, Democrats, or Independents. By registering with a particular party, citizens can vote in only that party's primary. But on Election Day, voters can vote for whomever they want, no matter what their party **affiliation** is.

caucuses select delegates who support a specific candidate. This is a public process. There is no private voting. The delegates then represent the people at county, state, and national conventions.

National Conventions

Have you ever watched a national convention on television? While it appears, at times, to be quite a celebration, it is also a working session for its attendees. At a party's political convention, its platform is adopted. This allows the party to have a unified voice. For example, the party will state its position on controversial topics, such as tax increases or budget cuts. At a national convention, parties endorse their presidential and vice presidential candidates, bringing them together as running mates. The highlight of each party's national convention is the acceptance speeches by its candidates.

Republican National Convention, Chicago, June 2, 1880

General Election Day

In the United States, general elections are held for national offices on the same day every two years—the first Tuesday following the first Monday of November. For example, if November 1 falls on a Monday, Election Day will be on November 2. However, if November 1 falls on a Tuesday, Election Day will be on the following Tuesday, November 8.

Voters do not elect officials for the same offices each year. Specifically, the president of the United States is elected every four years. One-third of United States senators are elected every two years for six-year terms, and United States representatives are elected every two years for two-year terms.

In general elections, citizens can vote for anyone running for a specific office. They are not restricted by their party affiliation as they are in primary elections.

At the end of Election Day, votes are counted. The candidate with the most votes wins the popular vote. However, if the election is for the president and vice president, the popular vote is not the final vote. The Electoral College casts the final vote. You will learn more about the Electoral College in chapter 5.

In state elections, the governor, who is the state leader, and legislators are elected. A governor is usually elected every four years. In New Hampshire and Vermont, however, the governor serves for only two years before standing for reelection.

The state legislators, who serve two- or four-year terms, make state laws while representing their local communities. In some states, judges are also elected. The lengths of their terms can vary.

Many ballots contain state-level issues. These include state-level education, road construction, and special programs for people in need.

Elections are also held at the local level. Citizens vote for new mayors, council representatives, school board members, and law enforcement officials. Many local issues are also voted on and decided.

Sometimes special elections must be held when there are ties to be broken, special issues to be resolved, or officials to be replaced. Many of these elections are held on days other than Election Day.

Republican gubernatorial candidate Arnold Schwarzenegger at a rally in Sacramento, California, days before the 2003 recall election in which he became the state's governor

Political Campaigns
Meeting the Candidates

Who runs for political office? Let's meet the candidates.

Types of Candidates

There are two types of candidates. Recruited candidates are the first type. These candidates are encouraged to run for office because other people in the political party think they would make good elected officials. While recruited candidates often have the support of sponsors, they may be expected to adopt the party's point of view and represent specific party concerns.

Self-starters are the second type of candidate. These candidates have a strong interest in the political process. Sometimes self-starters are called *whirlybirds* since they enter a political path by themselves. Perhaps you or one of your classmates is a self-starter. Ambitious young people often run for class offices.

Abraham Lincoln

One of the most famous self-starters was Abraham Lincoln. He lost many political races. Of course, he won a few, including the presidential election in 1860. Lincoln entered his first race as soon as he was old enough to be a candidate. About his numerous losses, he once stated, "I feel like the boy who stumped his toe. I am too big to cry and too badly hurt to laugh."

Reaching the Voters

The process of running for office is called *campaigning*. The candidates must convince people to vote for them. The candidates reach voters several ways.

Advertising

Advertising is one way candidates reach voters. Advertising is paid communication through television, magazines, radio, newspapers, and the Internet.

The goal of advertising is to persuade. Candidates try to convince citizens to vote for them. They place ads in local newspapers, on television, and on the radio. Advertising can be expensive. Money must be raised to pay for this form of communication.

FREE SOIL CANDIDATES FOR
PRESIDENT AND VICE-PRESIDENT.

Support a Candidate

Design a campaign ad to run in your local school paper. Who is the candidate? What office is the candidate seeking? What is the candidate's message?

Public Relations

Public relations (PR) is another form of communication. Public relations people help the public understand the candidate. A PR person sets up speaking opportunities

18

with potential supporters, sends out news releases about the candidate's platform, or invites the press to attend functions at which the candidate will be appearing. Public relations is about image. PR professionals work closely with the media to spread their candidates' messages and to make sure that the candidate is seen in a positive light.

Home Visits

Has a candidate ever come to your home? Many candidates make door-to-door visits, introducing themselves to the voters in the house. Candidates listen to concerns. They ask for the residents' votes. It would be hard for presidential candidates to visit many homes, but many local candidates use this method to reach out to voters. Candidates often leave brochures or other campaign literature explaining their **stand** on important issues.

Debates

Candidates appear on television, but not just in advertisements. Have you ever watched a **debate** on television? Individuals running for a specific office discuss important issues with one another. A **moderator** often asks questions. Each candidate has a **predetermined** amount of time to respond. By listening to debates, voters can compare the candidates' viewpoints.

The first televised debate was between Vice President Richard Nixon (left) and Senator John F. Kennedy (right) in 1960.

Rallies

When candidates gather many of their supporters together in one place, it is known as a **rally**. A candidate uses the energy of the group to build support for his campaign. Entertainment and refreshments are usually provided. The highlight of the rally is a speech given by the candidate. Rallies are often good PR opportunities for candidates. Local newspapers and television stations often report on rally activity.

Republican presidential candidate Herbert Hoover at a political rally, New York, 1928

Internet

Because many U.S. citizens now have access to computers and the Internet, candidates are exploring the use of Web sites to reach voters. The sites often include personal information about the candidates, their stand on issues, and how they plan to serve the voting community. Voters can ask questions or voice concerns through the site.

Campaign Costs

Running for political office can be expensive. There are many costs associated with campaigning— advertising, banners, television time, brochures, campaign headquarters, printing, consultants, travel, and more. Where does the money come from?

Hard Money, Soft Money, and PACs

In the 1992 presidential campaign, Texas billionaire Ross Perot spent $65 million of his personal money in an attempt to win votes. For his money, he received 19 percent of the vote, or about 19 million votes, at a cost of more than $3 per vote!

Our legislators have created laws that control the amount of money that can be raised for and spent on political campaigns.

Candidates for federal offices are limited in the amount of money they can receive from individuals and corporations. This funding is called *hard money*, and the limits are $1,000 for an individual contribution and $5,000 for a corporate or special interest group contribution.

Contributions beyond this amount can be made, however, but they must go to the political parties instead of to the individual candidates. These contributions are called *soft money*.

How do special interest groups contribute to political campaigns? Some set up Political Action Committees (PACs), which are used by organizations that want to persuade candidates to support their ideas. For example, the National Association of Home Builders has a PAC that gives money to the candidate it feels will pass laws that will favor the construction industry. The committees collect money from members of their organizations and friends. They then contribute the funding to candidates of their choice through their respective political parties.

The government may also contribute to a candidate's campaign through matching funds. For example, if a candidate raises $5 million, the government contributes $5 million, as long as campaign-financing regulations are followed.

First Stops: Iowa and New Hampshire

The stage for the presidential election is set at the Iowa caucuses and the New Hampshire primary election. The Iowa caucuses have traditionally been the first measure of how well each candidate will do in his or her bid for a party's nomination. One week later, the primary in New Hampshire often narrows the pool of candidates even further. Candidates who don't receive many votes in either of these states often drop out of the race.

Emerging party winners often receive more national media attention, an increase in television coverage, a boost in campaign funding, and momentum to carry them into the remaining primary showdowns.

Other parts of the United States have expressed interest in being first in the process. In 2004, the District of Columbia held an unofficial primary on January 13, a full two weeks before New Hampshire's primary.

> "As Iowa and New Hampshire go, so goes the nation" is an old saying that reflects the importance of the caucus and primary process.

Democratic presidential candidate Al Gore and his wife Tipper at the New Hampshire Primary in 2000

Chapter 4

Voting
Choosing Representatives

V oting is one way that all citizens of the United States can contribute to their community and country. It is how they select their leaders—in schools, communities, states, and the nation. It is also a way to voice their opinions on issues that are important.

Voting is not new. The ancient Greeks voted 2500 years ago to select their leaders. They used a voting method that has been used many times. They raised their hands to cast their votes.

The Romans were one of the first to use a secret ballot system about 2000 years ago. The ballot system allows people to vote in private. It is the system that we use today for public elections.

Who Can Vote?

Today, all U.S. citizens—American-born or **naturalized**—who are 18 years of age or older can vote in U.S. elections. But that was not always the case.

At one time, only white men who owned land were allowed to vote. This was not a true representation of the nation's citizens. If people were poor and did not own land, they could not vote. If they were women, they had no voice. If they were of African American descent, their opinions did not matter. Even Native Americans, who were the first to live in America, did not have the right to vote. If people could not read or write, they could not vote. It took 200 years to give all citizens the right to vote. It took 200 years for all voices to be heard.

23

Elizabeth Cady Stanton (1815–1902)

Although she did not live to see women secure the right to vote, Elizabeth Cady Stanton was instrumental in fighting for women's rights, including the right to vote.

As a child, Elizabeth Cady Stanton learned that girls didn't have the same rights or opportunities as boys. Because she was a female, she wasn't allowed to go to college. While she studied law with her father who was a judge, she was not allowed to practice it because of her sex.

Stanton was one of the authors of the "Declaration of Rights of the Women of the United States," which was presented by Susan B. Anthony during the U.S. centennial celebration in Washington, D.C., in 1876. With Matilda Joslyn Gage, Stanton wrote the *Woman's Bible* and headed the National Woman **Suffrage** Association. She collaborated with Anthony on the first three volumes of *A History of Woman Suffrage*.

Stanton's daughter, Harriot Stanton Blatch, carried on Stanton's work after her death in 1902.

Registering to Vote

The first step in voting is registering. Once U.S. citizens reach the age of 18, they are eligible to vote and can complete registration forms. At this time, they may be asked if they want to register with a particular political party.

In 1993, Congress passed a bill, known as the Motor-Voter bill, making it easier to register to vote. This law allows citizens 18 years of age or older to register to vote when they apply for or renew their driver's licenses.

Visitors to the United States, noncitizens, and individuals in prison cannot vote. They do not have the right.

Voter registration information is stored in a special office, and the records are computerized. The registrar or auditor is responsible for knowing who is registered to vote in the area. When people go to a polling place to vote, their names will appear on a list of voters for that **precinct** who are registered to vote in the election.

Who "Really" Votes?

Unfortunately, not everyone who can vote actually does vote. The people most likely to vote on Election Day are senior citizens, homeowners, married couples, individuals with advanced college degrees, and those with higher incomes.

According to the U.S. **Census** Bureau for the 2000 presidential election, 86 percent of registered voters actually voted. (The highest rate recorded was in 1968, when 91 percent of registered voters actually voted, and the lowest was in 1996, when only 82 percent showed up at the polls.)

Also, not everyone elegible to vote registers. In 2000, only 60 percent of citizens of voting age were registered to vote. Of those who were registered and did not vote, one in five said they were too busy.

Voting Percentages

Let's apply the 2000 voting percentages to a classroom of 30 students. If 60 percent of the students registered, 18 could vote. Of those 18, only 15 would actually vote. Do those 15 speak for the entire class?

When election officials announce the percentage of voter turnout for a city, county, state, or the nation, they are referring to the percent of eligible voters, not just the registered voters. In most general elections, only about 55 percent of all eligible voters do vote. For example, Wyoming had 99 percent of their registered voters turn out for the 2000 elections. That sounds terrific, but it takes on a completely different meaning when you learn that only 51 percent of eligible voters are registered. That means that only a little more than half of the eligible voters actually voted.

Casting the Vote

On Election Day, registered voters report to their assigned polling places. This might be in a school, library, church, community center, or other building located near the voters' homes. Most registered voters receive information prior to Election Day telling them where they should report and the hours the polling places will be open. Most polling locations are open from early morning before most people go to work until late in the evening after most people's workdays are over. Election officials try to accommodate the voters' schedules.

Upon arriving, each voter must report to an election official. An election official may ask the voter to sign in. The voter's personal information is compared to the information on the voter-registration list. In most cases, some form of identification is required.

It is now time to select your government representatives. It is time to vote!

Kids Voting U.S.A.

You might not be old enough to officially vote, but you are old enough to visit your polling place, learn about the election process, and maybe even cast an "unofficial" vote.

One group that encourages student involvement on Election Day is Kids Voting U.S.A. at **www.kidsvotingusa.org**. This program teaches the importance of being informed and the responsibilities of voting.

The founders of the program discovered while visiting Costa Rica that voter turnout is 80 percent in this country. In Costa Rica, parents take their children along to the polling places and allow them to learn firsthand the importance of civic duty.

Recording Your Candidate Selections

Voting equipment varies. Election officials are searching for recording methods that are more consistent from location to location and from state to state.

Marksense Ballots

One method of recording a voter's choices is the marksense ballot. These cards are printed with candidates' names. Next to each name is a shape—a circle, an oval, a rectangle, or an incomplete arrow. With pencils or black markers, voters fill in the empty shape or complete the arrow next to the name of the candidate for whom they wish to vote. A computer reads the darkest

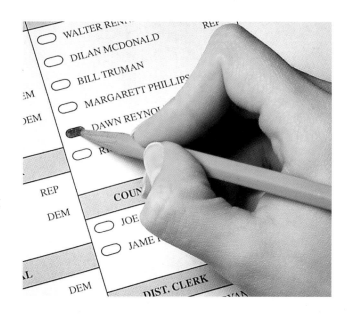

marks and reports the results. Marksense balloting is sometimes referred to as *optical scanning*. In the 1996 election, approximately 25 percent of all polling places used this method of voting.

Standardized Tests

You may already be an expert at marksense balloting! It uses the same method of marking choices that many standardized-testing companies use. When you fill in the shape to represent your best choice for an answer, you are preparing your answer sheet to be read by a computer. It is the same way that your parents may cast their votes for the president of the United States! You are a voter-in-training.

Mechanical-Lever Machines

Mechanical-lever machines are another way to record votes. Each candidate's name is positioned below a lever, and voters move these levers from one position to another to cast their votes. Only one lever for each group of candidates can be moved. The mechanical-lever machine is activated when the voter enters the machine and pulls the handle to close the privacy curtain. Votes are officially recorded when the voter exits the machine by pulling the handle to open the curtain.

The first mechanical-lever machine was called the Myers Automatic Booth. It was used in Lockport, New York, in 1892. Lever machines were installed in almost every major city in the United States by 1930. More than half of the country's votes were being cast on these machines by 1960. With the introduction of new technologies, such as marksense ballots/optical scanning devices, manufacturers of mechanical-level machines stopped making them. In 1996, only 21 percent of voters used the mechanical equipment to cast their votes. As parts on these machines break and cannot be replaced, other voting devices will take the place of the remaining machines.

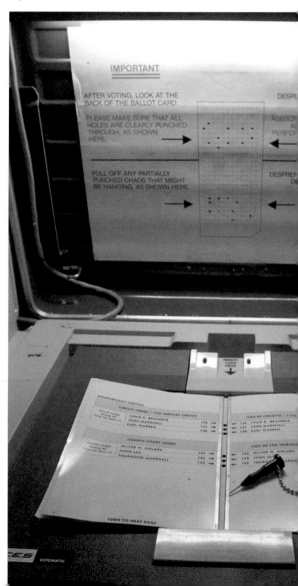

Punch Cards

One of the most popular methods of recording votes is the punch-card system, which uses a card and a small clipboard-sized device. With a special punching device called a *stylus*, voters punch holes in the cards next to their candidates' names. Votes are counted using a computer device to read the holes. In the 1996 presidential election, more than 33 percent of registered voters in the United States used the punch-card system.

Paper Ballots

Dating back to 1789 in New York, the paper ballot system uses official ballot paper on which the names of all candidates are printed. Changes came about in the late 1800s when the country adopted the secret ballot. Voters record their choices, in private, by marking the boxes next to the candidate. They then drop their ballot into the ballot box.

In 1996, less than two percent of registered voters cast votes using the paper ballot system. Paper ballots are mostly found in small communities and rural areas. They are also used for **absentee balloting** throughout the country.

Direct-Recording Electronic Technology

The most recent method of voting uses the direct-recording electronic (DRE) technology. It is an electronic version of the old, mechanical-lever systems. Voters use touch screens, push buttons, or similar devices to note their selections. In 1996, almost eight percent of the registered voters in the United States used some type of DRE voting system.

Absentee Ballots

Voters who cannot physically go to their designated polling locations on Election Day can vote using absentee ballots. Absentee voters include individuals who are traveling, members of the military, and people confined to their homes with health limitations. The rules for requesting and submitting absentee ballots are different for each state.

Counting the Voices

When the polls close, election officials count the votes and the results are reported. Paper ballots are counted by hand. Computer-aided voting methods are finalized. Election officials send results to the appropriate offices at the city, county, state, and national levels.

These results are reported through television, newspapers, radio, and the Internet. For national elections, reporters are discouraged from reporting results from the East Coast that might influence voters on the West Coast before their polls close.

The popular vote goes to the candidate with the most votes, but for candidate teams running for president and vice president of the United States, the popular vote may not be enough. These two offices are determined by the Electoral College.

Chapter 5

History of Voting
Hearing One Voice at a Time

Ballots and voting equipment list the names of the candidates for president and vice president, but voters do not vote directly for these positions. They vote, instead, for electors who have promised to support these candidates.

Today each state has a predetermined number of electors, ranging from 3 to 54. This number equals the total number of senators and representatives each state sends to Congress. The electors make up a group called the Electoral College, which is described in Article II of the Constitution of the United States.

House of Representatives

The number of representatives that each state sends to Congress is based on the state's population. The population is determined every ten years when a new survey is taken by the United States Census Bureau.

U.S. House of Representatives

Today, there are 538 total electoral votes. To win, a candidate needs 270 electoral votes. It is possible, however, that no candidate will receive the necessary number of votes. If this happens, the House of Represenatatives selects the president.

STATE OF ALABAMA
CERTIFICATE OF VOTE
ELECTORAL COLLEGE
2000

We, the undersigned, being duly elected Electors for President and Vice President of the United States of America, for the State of Alabama, at the General Election held on Tuesday, November 7, 2000, pursuant to the Constitution and laws of the United States and of this State, certify that the following candidates for President and Vice President received the following number of votes, by ballot, at the meeting of Electors held December 18, 2000, at the State Capitol in Montgomery, Alabama.

FOR PRESIDENT OF THE UNITED STATES
GEORGE W. BUSH
NUMBER OF ELECTOR VOTES: 9

FOR VICE PRESIDENT OF THE UNITED STATES
DICK CHENEY
NUMBER OF ELECTOR VOTES: 9

ELAINE LITTLE
MELBA PETERS
MARTHA STOKES
JEAN SULLIVAN
EDGAR WELDEN

In Testimony Whereof, I have hereunto set my hand and affixed the Great Seal of the State of Alabama at the State Capitol in the City of Montgomery on this Eighteenth day of December, 2000.

JIM BENNETT
SECRETARY OF STATE

See You in December

While Election Day is the first Tuesday following the first Monday in November, the actual election does not take place until December, when members of the Electoral College meet in their own states and cast votes. The votes are then sealed and sent to the U.S. Senate.

Early Elections

When the Founders of this country first gathered, they had many questions as to how the president should be elected.

★ Should Congress decide who should be president?

★ Should state legislators select the president, giving states power in a federal system?

★ Should the president be selected by the people in a time when communication and transportation was limited?

★ Should there be a lottery system to determine which members of Congress have voting power?

In September 1787, the Founders opted to compromise, and the idea of electors and the Electoral College was born. Article II of the Constitution states how the number of electors is determined. While the number of electors given to each state is predetermined, each state decides how to select its electors.

As the hero of the Revolutionary War, George Washington was elected the first president of the United States by the country's electors. John Q. Adams became his vice president. The first inauguration was held at Federal Hall in New York City in 1789.

In future elections, the country's leaders discovered flaws in the system. There were candidates from two political parties for the election of 1796. Electors selected a president, John Q. Adams, from one party and a vice president, Thomas Jefferson, from another party. How did this happen? Electors did not vote separately for the two offices. Thomas Jefferson was actually a presidential candidate, but he had the second highest number of votes, which under the Constitution at that time, made him the country's vice president.

The Three-Fifths Compromise

In 1787, states in the North differed strongly with states in the South regarding issues related to slavery. Some states felt that all people—including slaves—should be counted when determining a state's population, and therefore its representation in the Electoral College. Other states disagreed. Delegates at the Constitutional Convention came up with a compromise, counting each slave as three-fifths of a person.

President and Vice President

In early elections, candidates for president and vice president did not run together on the same **ticket**, as they do today. Everyone was on one ballot, and the electors voted for two people. The man with the most votes was named president. The man with the next highest number of votes became vice president. The 12th Amendment changed this so there was a separate ballot for president and vice president. Electors still cast two votes, but now they cast one vote for president and one for vice president.

Here are a few other noteworthy elections in our country's history.

1824 Four candidates ran for president. The winner of both the popular vote and the electoral vote was Andrew Jackson. He did not have enough electoral votes for a majority, however. Under the Constitution, when no one candidate captures the majority electoral vote, the House of Representatives selects the president. The House did not choose Jackson. They selected the runner-up, John Q. Adams.

Adams

Jackson

1860 The issue of slavery caused a division among states and political parties. Four candidates from four opposing parties ran for president. Abraham Lincoln won the election with only 40 percent of the popular vote. His election angered the people of the South, and 11 states withdrew from the Union. Lincoln refused to accept their withdrawal, and the country went to war.

1876 The popular vote was won by Samuel J. Tilden. With electoral votes from three states still to be counted, he was one elector short of becoming president. His opponent was Rutherford B. Hayes. Both Tilden and Hayes were claiming they won the votes from the three remaining states. A special Electoral Commission was formed to determine the votes. The Commission awarded the electoral votes for the three states to Hayes, and he became president.

1888 At issue was a tariff, a tax added to goods imported from other countries. Incumbent Democratic President Grover Cleveland sided with consumers, opposing the tariff. His opponent, Republican Benjamin Harrison, sided with and was supported by big business. They favored the tax because it made American products look more attractive. Cleveland won the popular vote, but Harrison won the majority of electoral votes.

2000 Voters did not know the outcome of the 2000 presidential election between candidates George W. Bush and Albert Gore until 35 days after their votes were cast. All eyes were on Florida, the state that would determine the winner with its 25 electoral votes. The popular votes were so close that they were recounted several times. On December 12, the U.S. Supreme Court stopped the counting. George W. Bush won Florida and the election.

Present Electoral College

According to the Federal Election Commission, the current Electoral College operates as follows.

★ Each state is given a number of electors equal to the number of its U.S. senators plus the number of its U.S. representatives.

★ The political parties in each state provide to the state's chief election official a list of individuals who will support their candidate for president. The number submitted equals the number of state electoral votes. Members of Congress and employees of the federal government cannot be electors.

★ After party primaries and caucuses, the major parties nominate their candidates for president and vice president at their national conventions. Candidates' names appear on the ballots in the individual states.

★ On Election Day, the people in each state vote for president and vice president. Their vote determines which set of electors will represent the state.

★ On the first Monday following the second Wednesday of December, each state's electors meet in their respective state capitals and cast their electoral votes—one for president and one for vice president. The candidate with the most popular votes in each state receives that state's electoral votes. There are two exceptions—Maine and Nebraska. These two states can split the electoral votes between the candidates.

★ The electoral votes are then sealed and sent to the Senate, where the results are read on January 6. The candidate for president with the most electoral votes is declared president if the majority figure is reached. The vice presidential candidate with the absolute majority of electoral votes is declared vice president. If a majority is not reached, the U.S. House of Representatives selects the president from the top three candidates. Each state casts only one vote and a majority is required. For vice president, the U.S. Senate selects from the top two candidates for that office.

★ At noon on January 20, the elected president and vice president are sworn into office.

Electoral College Votes by State or District for 2004 and 2008

Alabama	9	Louisiana	9	Oklahoma	7
Alaska	3	Maine	4	Oregon	7
Arizona	10	Maryland	10	Pennsylvania	21
Arkansas	6	Massachusetts	12	Rhode Island	4
California	55	Michigan	17	South Carolina	8
Colorado	9	Minnesota	10	South Dakota	3
Connecticut	7	Mississippi	6	Tennessee	11
Delaware	3	Missouri	11	Texas	34
District of Columbia	3	Montana	3	Utah	5
Florida	27	Nebraska	5	Vermont	3
Georgia	15	Nevada	5	Virginia	13
Hawaii	4	New Hampshire	4	Washington	11
Idaho	4	New Jersey	15	West Virginia	5
Illinois	21	New Mexico	5	Wisconsin	10
Indiana	11	New York	31	Wyoming	3
Iowa	7	North Carolina	15		
Kansas	6	North Dakota	3	**Total**	**538**
Kentucky	8	Ohio	20	**Needed to win**	**270**

Future of the Electoral College

In the more than 200 years of this nation's history, Congress has been presented with more than 700 proposals to change or eliminate the role of the Electoral College. These requests number more than requests to change any other section of the Constitution.

Those against the Electoral College claim that it is outdated. The winner of the popular vote may lose the electoral vote and the election. Individual voters may choose not to vote, thinking that their voices are not being heard. The process of determining the number of electoral votes per state is based on a census taken once every ten years and may not truly reflect current population statistics.

Those in favor of the Electoral College believe it has worked well in the past. Candidates must campaign in each individual state and not just those with the highest population. It eliminates the need to do a recount of the entire country's votes in the case of a close popular vote.

An amendment to the Constitution would be required to eliminate the Electoral College. Two steps are required to pass such an amendment. First, two-thirds of both the House and Senate must vote in favor of the change. Then, state legislatures in 38 states—representing three-fourths of the country—must **ratify** it.

Debating Your Future

Should the Electoral College remain or be eliminated? Divide your class into two groups. Research both sides of the issue. Present your points of view to the other group. Did you provide supporting facts? Were you persuasive in your arguments? How did your audience react?

Chapter 6

Political Parties
People and Platforms

When you register to vote, you may be asked to select a political party to which you want to belong. What is a political party? It is a group of voters who share similar beliefs about government and important issues. Each political party has a platform, or a set of ideas and issues.

Political parties help their candidates during the campaign. They raise money, recruit volunteers, share expenses, and offer support to candidates within the party.

Today, there are two major parties—the Democrats and the Republicans. But it was not always this way.

Federalist Party

The first president of the United States was neither a Democrat nor a Republican. He was a Federalist, one of the first political parties of the United States. Federalists believed in a strong, central government. They thought states should have less power than the federal government.

The opposing party at that time was the Democratic-Republican Party. This party believed that states should hold the most power, not the federal government. In 1840, the Democratic-Republican Party became the Democratic Party.

The Federalist Party went through a few changes, too, during this time. The National Republican Party first replaced it. It then became the Whig Party. Some of its members—and some Democrats, too—separated and formed a new party in 1854. This became the Republican Party that we know today.

Both parties have modified their beliefs over time. Here is what they believe today.

History of the Donkey Mascot

While the Democrats have never officially adopted the donkey as their symbol, the party has used various donkey designs in its campaigns, starting in 1828. Thomas Nast, a famous political cartoonist, used the donkey in an 1870 *Harper's Weekly* cartoon. The donkey was well established by 1880 as the mascot for the Democratic Party. The donkey is a symbol characterized as humble, homely, smart, courageous, and lovable.

History of the Elephant Mascot

Cartoonist Thomas Nast had a hand in the development of the Republican elephant symbol. It first appeared in *Harper's Weekly* in 1874, a few years after the Democratic donkey. Republicans believe that the elephant represents a dignified, strong, and intelligent party.

The Democratic Party

In general, the Democratic Party is the **liberal** party. It believes that a large central government is necessary to make laws and meet social challenges, including the welfare of all its citizens. This party wants states to have less power than the federal government.

The Republican Party

Republicans are thought to be more **conservative** in their approach to government and change. They want the federal government to be less involved, giving more power to the individual states. They want individuals to be responsible for their own well-being. The Republican Party is sometimes called the Grand Old Party, or GOP.

"Third Party" Players

People and their feelings about issues do not always fit into neat categories. While some citizens feel strongly about the political platforms of the Democratic and Republican Parties, others do not.

Some voters choose to be independent voters, belonging to neither party. They make election choices based only on the candidates and their views and not on their party affiliation.

Many people feel strongly about certain issues that don't match either party. They may form their own political party. Any party that is not Democratic or Republican is called a *third party*. Perhaps you have heard of the Green Party. In the 2000 presidential election, this party supported Ralph Nader for president. The Green Party has a commitment to the environment and no interest in taking "green" money from corporations to support government. Third-place Nader received about three percent of the popular vote in the general election and no electoral votes.

There are many other political parties, each representing a group of people with similar goals or feelings.

2000 Presidential Election Results by State

Bush (R)
Gore (D)

Chapter 7

Being a Citizen
Having a Voice Before You Vote

You may not be old enough to vote, but you are old enough to be an active member of your community and to have a voice about issues facing you and your world.

Start in Your Own Backyard

What can you do to improve your community and, therefore, the world? It takes more than money to make a difference. It takes people.

Look around you. Is there trash in a park to be picked up or a stream to be cleaned? Organize a group of friends to help you beautify an area.

Does a neighbor need a helping hand? Rake your neighbors' leaves or shovel their sidewalks when it snows.

Is there a small child who needs help reading? Volunteer at your local library to read books to children.

Are there animals that need care? Ask your local animal shelter if you can help. Perhaps you can walk the dogs or play with the kittens.

These may seem like small tasks, but they are important to the world in which you live. And they can be done in your own community. Making your world a better place starts with you.

Get to Know the Issues

By reading this book, you have taken an important step in educating yourself about your government and the important role that you and all citizens of the United States play in the welfare of this country. But learning about the issues and candidates before you vote requires more research. You can find current information in newspapers, magazines, on the Internet, and on television.

If you make it your goal to learn a little bit each day about your world—from your local community to a country on another continent—you will become a more informed citizen and, some day, a more informed voter!

Write to Your Representative

Politicians represent you and, therefore, need to know what YOU think. Perhaps you would like to share with them your thoughts about your school and your education. Maybe you would like to thank your local representative for the money he or she was able to **allocate** for a special program in your community. Do you have a concern or question about something? Write to your representative!

Support Voting Activities

You might not be able to vote for your favorite candidates right now, but you can still support them. You can make copies, hand out flyers, pass out buttons, and hang posters. Perhaps you can help at the polling place on Election Day. Just contact the local headquarters for your candidate or your local election headquarters.

Raise Money for a Cause

Fund-raising is a way to collect money for a special cause. Your school may already do this. Does your school save store receipts or labels and boxtops from products to buy equipment?

Your class may have a cause it would like to support. For example, you can raise money to buy new books to donate to waiting rooms at local doctors' offices and hospitals. Perhaps you could raise money to pay for taxi services to drive senior citizens to polling places on Election Day. You could sponsor a holiday basket for a needy family in a neighboring community or buy seeds to start a community garden to support the efforts of the local food bank.

Internet Connections and Related Readings

for Elections and Political Parties

www2.lhric.org/pocantico/election/election.htm
Discover step-by-step how a president is elected. The site also includes other kid-friendly sites to visit.

www.democrats.org
Follow Democratic candidates as they prepare for election. Read about issues that concern the members of the party.

www.fec.gov/citizen-guide.html
The Federal Elections Commission has a section on how elections work that includes information about voting systems, the Electoral College, and voter registration.

www.takeyourkidstovote.org/youth/index.htm
Click on the elementary and middle school links for ideas about how you can be involved even if you can't vote yet.

www.kidsnewsroom.com/election/election.asp
The Kids Newsroom answers many questions you may have about the election process.

www.kidsvotingusa.org/students/students.asp
Kids Voting U.S.A. is a nonpartisan organization that educates and engages young people in voting. Click on any of the buttons for online activities and other links.

www.rnc.org

Follow Republican candidates as they prepare for election. Read about issues that concern the members of the party.

www.uselectionatlas.org

This site provides voting statistics for general elections throughout history. Find out how voters in your state have voted over the years.

bensguide.gpo.gov

Enter Ben's Guide to U.S. Government for Kids and explore the election process and other interesting topics that relate to the U.S. government.

www.multied.com/elections/index.html

History Central takes a look at the history of presidential elections, disputed elections, the Electoral College, and election statistics.

Our Constitution by Linda Carlson Johnson. This book describes the creation of the document that sets out the rules of government for our country. Milbrook, 1992. [RL 5.6 IL 3–6] (4695306 HB)

Our Elections by Richard Steins. The democratic process is clearly illustrated in a description of the voting process in the United States. The book relates the unique features of the presidential election, discusses history-making elections, and explains how to write to Congress and work on campaigns. Milbrook, 1994. [RL 4.5 IL 3–6] (4930806 HB)

The letters *RL* in the brackets indicate the reading level of the book listed. *IL* indicates the approximate interest level. Perfection Learning's catalog numbers are included for your ordering convenience. *HB* indicates hardcover.

Glossary

absentee balloting (ab suhn TEE BAL uht ing) process by which voters who are unable to vote in person can send their vote to the official election bureau in another form

affiliation (uh fil ee AY shuhn) connection to or membership in a group

allocate (AL oh kayt) to give something to a particular person or group

amendment (uh MEND muhnt) addition or change to a bill or the Constitution

association (uh soh see AY shuhn) group of people joined together for a purpose

ballot (BAL uht) piece of paper or card on which someone can record a vote

candidate (KAN di dayt) someone who runs for election for a political office or an official position

census (SEN suhs) relating to an official count of a population

conservative (kuhn SER vuh tiv) a person favoring gradual change, seeking to preserve traditional institutions

convention (kuhn VEN shuhn) meeting of the delegates (see separate glossary entry) of a political party for the purpose of selecting candidates (see separate glossary entry)

debate (di BAYT) organized discussion of opinions or ideas

delegate (DEL uh guht) someone chosen to represent or given the authority to act on behalf of another person, group, or organization

dictator (DIK tay ter) leader who rules a country with absolute power, usually by force

electoral (i LEK tor uhl) relating to or involving elections, electors, or voters

eligible (EL i juh buhl) meeting the requirements to do something

global (GLOH buhl) relating to or happening throughout the world

liberal (LIB er uhl) a person favoring progress and reform, especially regarding the protection of civil liberties

literacy (LIT er uh see) ability to read and write at a competent level

moderator (MOD er ay ter) someone who leads discussion in a debate

monarch (MON ark) someone, especially a king or queen, who rules a country for life by inherited right

monarchy (MON ark ee) political system in which a country is ruled by a monarch (see separate glossary entry)

naturalized (NACH er uh leyezd) having been granted citizenship by a country other than the one in which you were born

nominate (NOM in ayt) to suggest someone for appointment or election

participatory (par TIS uh puh tor ee) relating to all persons taking part in something

platform (PLAT form) publicly announced policies and promises of a party seeking election

poll tax (pohl taks) flat-rate amount of money that must be paid by individuals in order to vote

precinct (PRE sinkt) small voting district of a city or town

predetermined (pre di TER muhnd) having been decided in advance

primary election (PRI mair ee i LEK shun) election in which members of a party choose delegates (see separate glossary entry) who will choose the party's candidate (see separate glossary entry) at a political convention (see separate glossary entry)

public relations (PUB lik ri LAY shuhnz) practice of establishing, maintaining, or improving a favorable relationship between a person or group and the public

rally (RAL ee) large meeting or gathering of people, usually organized by a movement or political party and intended to inspire and generate enthusiasm among those present

ratify (RAT uh feye) to give formal approval to something

recall (REE kawl) to remove an elected official from office before his or her term is up

referendum (ref er REN duhm) vote by the entire voting population on a specific question brought up by the government or similar body

right (reyet) freedom or privilege to do something

self-starter (self START er) someone with the initiative and motivation to work without needing help or supervision

slogan (SLOH gun) short catchy phrase used to identify something or someone

stand (stand) opinion

suffrage (SUHF rij) relating to the right (see separate glossary entry) to vote in public elections

ticket (TIK uht) list of candidates (see separate glossary entry) put forward by one party or group in an election

Index